FAMOUS SCIENTISTS

LEGENDS AND GAME CHANGERS

BY ELSIE OLSON

eureka!

Eureka!

Eureka! books turn real stories into unforgettable experiences. This nonfiction imprint sparks curiosity, encourages critical thinking, and engages middle-grade readers. *Eureka!* books empower young minds to explore the stories of the real world, one fascinating fact at a time. Unravel the power of knowledge and lifelong learning with *Eureka!*

This edition first published in 2026 by Bellwether Media, Inc.

Library of Congress Cataloging-in-Publication Data

LC record for Famous Scientists available at: https://lccn.loc.gov/2025019768

Editor: Betsy Rathburn   Series Designer: Jeffrey Kollock   Book Designer: Josh Brink

Printed in the United States of America, North Mankato, MN.

TABLE OF CONTENTS

SCIENCE HISTORY

Science is the study of the world around us through gathering evidence, experimenting, and testing theories. Throughout history, science has helped people survive. Ancient people used science to determine which plants were poisonous, which were good to eat, and which could treat illnesses. People studied the stars to learn when to plant and harvest crops and how to navigate around the world. They also used scientific concepts to construct strong buildings. Some still stand today!

Today's scientists continue to push our knowledge forward. Advanced technology helps them conduct experiments that build on the knowledge of the past. Scientists have helped humans explore the ocean floor, the insides of volcanoes, and even different planets. They have helped humans live healthier lives by curing diseases and developing stronger new crops. They have created new technologies that help make our lives better. Without science, the modern world we live in would not be possible!

TIMELINE

AROUND 3100 BCE–
Egypt is the center of anatomy knowledge for many centuries

1500s CE–
Nicolaus Copernicus creates the theory that Earth orbits the sun

1676
Antonie van Leeuwenhoek becomes the first person to view bacteria under a microscope

1796
Edward Jenner develops the world's first successful vaccine

1859
Charles Darwin publishes a book proposing the theories of natural selection and evolution

1912
Alfred Wegener proposes the theory that continents sit on moving plates

LATE 1950s
Charles Keeling develops a new way to measure carbon dioxide in the atmosphere

1971
Paul Murdin and Louise Webster discover black holes

1990
the Human Genome Project begins mapping human DNA

2024
NASA's Parker Solar Probe makes its closest approach to the sun

CHEMISTRY

Chemistry is the study of matter. It explores the structure, properties, and chemical makeup of different substances. Chemists have been responsible for major breakthroughs, including the discovery of new elements.

COMPUTER SCIENCE

Computer science is the study of computers. It explores how computers may be designed and used. Computer scientists research the uses of **artificial intelligence** (AI), create programming languages, develop computer security systems, and more.

PHYSICS

Physics is the study of how objects interact with one another. Physicists research the movement and energy created by matter. Important physics discoveries include how gravity works and how black holes form.

ASTRONOMY

Astronomy is the study of objects in outer space. Astronomers have made important discoveries about how the planets move around the solar system and how the universe first formed.

MORE SCIENCE, MORE SCIENTISTS!

EARTH AND CLIMATE SCIENCE

Earth and climate science is the study of Earth and its atmosphere. Scientists in this field have helped us better understand how Earth's landforms change over time and how human activity affects the planet's climate.

BIOLOGY

Biology is the study of living things. It includes the study of plants and animals, **microorganisms**, and genetics. Biologists are responsible for many major discoveries, including how plants and animals change over time and cures for deadly diseases.

MARY ANNING

Paleontology is the study of ancient life through fossils. Mary Anning was an English paleontologist who lived in the early 1800s. She developed an interest in fossils at a young age. When she was 12, she found her first dinosaur fossil along the coast of England. She found dozens more fossils during her lifetime, including one of the first pterosaur fossils!

JEAN PIAGET

Psychology is the study of the mind and behavior. Jean Piaget was a Swiss psychologist whose work focused on brain development. He proposed that children go through different stages of development as they grow. He believed that these stages influence how children gain knowledge. Piaget's research helped change the way children are taught in schools.

GERTRUDE B. ELION

Pharmacology is the study of medicine and how it affects living things. Gertrude B. Elion was an American pharmacologist whose work focused on treating disease. She helped develop life-saving treatments for leukemia, malaria, and many other illnesses. She won a Nobel Prize in 1988.

MARIA SIBYLLA MERIAN

Entomology is the study of insects. Entomologists study the relationships of insects with other organisms and their environments. Maria Sibylla Merian was a German entomologist who was born in the 1600s. She was one of the first people to document insect **metamorphosis**. She created groundbreaking illustrations of this process.

CHEMISTS

Marie Curie is famous for making incredible discoveries at a time when few women were allowed to work in science. Her work continues to impact science and medicine!

Marie Curie

LIFE IN POLAND

Curie was born in Poland in the 1860s. From a young age, she was a good student who loved learning. But her local university did not admit women at that time. Curie studied in secret.

LOVE AND SCIENCE

Eventually, Curie moved to Paris, France, to attend Sorbonne University. There, she studied physics, chemistry, and math. She also met a professor named Pierre Curie. They married in 1895 and began working on research together.

NEW DISCOVERIES

Curie studied the element uranium. Its atoms give off energy called **radiation**. Curie wanted to see if other elements did this, too. In 1898, she and Pierre discovered two new elements, radium and polonium. These also gave off radiation. In 1903, she and Pierre won the Nobel Prize in Physics for their discoveries. She was the first woman to win the Nobel Prize.

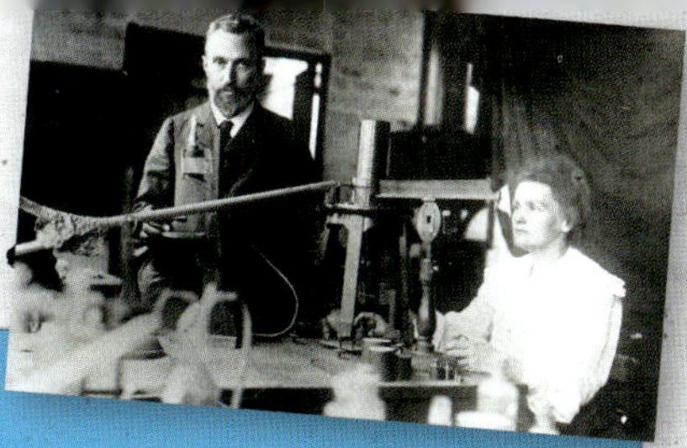

NEW INVENTIONS

In 1906, Pierre died unexpectedly. Curie continued her work. She won another Nobel Prize in 1911, this time in chemistry. In 1914, Curie invented a mobile X-ray machine. It was used during World War I. In 1932, Curie helped open the Radium Institute in Poland, the country that once banned her from studying science.

BORN: November 7, 1867, in Warsaw, Poland

DIED: July 4, 1934

EDUCATION: Sorbonne University

KNOWN FOR: discovered radium and polonium and invented mobile X-ray machines

AWARDS AND HONORS

- **1903** Nobel Prize in Physics
- **1911** Nobel Prize in Chemistry
- **1921** John Scott Medal

LIKE MOTHER, LIKE DAUGHTER

Curie's daughter Irène Joliot-Curie followed in her mother's footsteps and became a chemist. In 1935, she won the Nobel Prize in Chemistry.

TIMELINE

1891 moves to Paris to study physics

1898 discovers radium and polonium along with her husband, Pierre

1903 earns a doctorate in physics and is awarded a Nobel Prize

1906 becomes the first woman to teach at Sorbonne University

1932 helps open the Radium Institute in Poland

Louis Pasteur

French chemist Louis Pasteur spent most of his life studying microorganisms. He developed vaccines to cure deadly diseases. His work saves millions of lives every year.

GETTING STARTED

As a child, Pasteur loved drawing and painting. He went on to study science as an adult. In the late 1840s, Pasteur began working as a chemistry professor.

SAFER BEVERAGES

In 1854, Pasteur began studying **fermentation**, a chemical process used to make certain beverages. He discovered that it is caused by microorganisms such as bacteria and yeast. In 1862, Pasteur began developing a new process called pasteurization. Products are heated to a certain temperature. This removes harmful microorganisms. This new process made foods and drinks safer. We still use it today!

VACCINE DEVELOPMENT

Pasteur also used his work with bacteria to develop vaccines. In 1881, he created a vaccine for a deadly disease called anthrax. In 1885, his rabies vaccine cured a boy who had been bitten by a rabid dog. This was the first time a rabies patient had ever been cured. The success made Pasteur world-famous!

GERM THEORY

Pasteur also developed the germ theory of disease. This theory explains that bacteria causes many diseases. Before it was accepted, people believed bad smells caused disease.

TIMELINE

1842 graduates from Royal College of Besançon

1862 completes his first pasteurization test

LATER LIFE

In 1887, the Pasteur Institute was founded in Pasteur's honor. Its scientists continue to conduct important health research. Pasteur died in 1895. But he is still remembered today. His work has saved millions of lives and changed the way doctors practice medicine.

AWARDS AND HONORS

- 1856 Rumford Medal
- 1874 Copley Medal
- 1882 Albert Medal

BORN: December 27, 1822, in Dole, France

DIED: September 28, 1895

EDUCATION: Royal College of Besançon, École Normale Supérieure

KNOWN FOR: developed pasteurization and created vaccines for anthrax and rabies

1879 invents the first laboratory-created vaccine, which cures chicken cholera

1881 completes the first successful test of his anthrax vaccine

1885 cures rabies for the first time with his vaccine

Rosalind Franklin

Rosalind Franklin was a British scientist who took the first images of **DNA**, revealing its structure. Although she received little recognition during her lifetime, her work led to a better understanding of DNA.

CHEMISTRY WHIZ

As a teenager, Franklin knew she wanted to be a scientist. In 1938, she began studying chemistry at Newnham College. After graduating in 1941, she began researching the properties of coal. This work led to her earning her doctorate in 1945.

WORKING WITH X-RAYS

In the late 1940s, Franklin began working at a laboratory in Paris, France. There, she became an expert in **X-ray diffraction**. This process let her observe how X-rays interacted with the atoms in different materials. This revealed information about their structure.

PHOTO 51

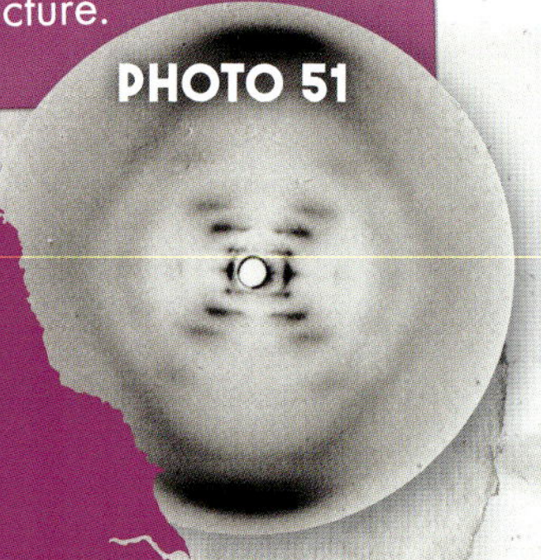

AWARDS AND HONORS

2008
Honorary Louisa Gross Horwitz Prize

TIMELINE

- **1945** earns a doctorate in physical chemistry from Newnham College
- **LATE 1940s** moves to Paris, where she learns the technique of X-ray diffraction
- **1952** takes the first pictures showing DNA has a double helix structure
- **1953** begins studying viruses at Birkbeck College
- **1962** scientists Francis Crick, James Watson, and Maurice Wilkins win the Nobel Prize for research based on Franklin's work

PHOTOGRAPHING DNA

In 1951, Franklin moved back to London. There, she used X-ray diffraction to study DNA. At the time, scientists knew little about DNA structure. In 1952, Franklin took Photo 51. This famous photo shows that DNA has a twisted ladder structure now known as a double helix. However, other scientists received credit for Franklin's discovery. Still, she kept working.

STUDYING VIROLOGY

In 1953, Franklin began focusing on studying viruses. Her work helped uncover the structure of **RNA**, paving the way for future vaccines. Today, many people recognize Franklin's contributions to the fields of chemistry and biology.

"Science and everyday life cannot and should not be separated."

—Rosalind Franklin

BORN: July 25, 1920, in London, England

DIED: April 16, 1958

EDUCATION: Newnham College, University of Cambridge

KNOWN FOR: took the first images of DNA showing its double helix structure

Katalin Karikó

Katalin Karikó is famous for helping develop a vaccine for COVID-19. This has saved millions of lives. One day, her work may be used to treat even more diseases.

EXPLORING BIOCHEMISTRY

Karikó was raised in a small Hungarian village. She loved science and nature as a child. She went on to study biology at the University of Szeged. In 1982, she earned a doctorate in biochemistry. After finishing school, she began conducting research professionally.

EXPLORING RNA

Karikó studied a molecule called RNA. RNA is found in every living cell. It carries instructions from DNA to create proteins. These proteins help build cells. This process is needed for life to exist. Karikó was interested in how RNA could be used to fight diseases.

FUTURE CURES

Karikó's mRNA process could one day be used to treat genetic diseases such as cystic fibrosis and Huntington's disease.

TIMELINE

1982 receives a doctorate in biochemistry from the University of Szeged

1985 moves to the United States

MOVING TO AMERICA

In 1985, Karikó moved to the United States. She began to focus her research on messenger RNA, or mRNA. In the late 1990s, Karikó studied how to use mRNA to treat diseases. In 2013, she began working with a **biotechnology** company to develop mRNA-based treatments.

THE COVID-19 PANDEMIC

In 2020, the COVID-19 virus caused a global **pandemic**. Karikó worked with a team to develop an mRNA-based vaccine to fight and prevent COVID-19. The vaccine worked! In 2023, Karikó and Drew Weissman won a Nobel Prize for their work.

AWARDS AND HONORS

- **2022** Novo Nordisk Prize
- **2023** Nobel Prize in Physiology or Medicine
- **2023** National Inventors Hall of Fame

BORN: January 17, 1955, in Kisújszállás, Hungary

EDUCATION: University of Szeged

KNOWN FOR: researched mRNA technology and developed a vaccine for COVID-19

2013 joins biotechnology company BioNTech

2020 helps develop a vaccine to treat COVID-19

2023 earns a Nobel Prize for her work in developing the COVID-19 vaccine

COMPUTER SCIENTISTS

Grace Hopper was an American computer scientist known for her work on early computer programming languages. Through decades of military service, she rose to the rank of rear admiral in the U.S. Navy.

Grace Hopper

EARLY LIFE

From a young age, Hopper showed an interest in technology. She enjoyed taking apart clocks in her family's home to see how they worked. In 1928, she earned degrees in mathematics and physics from Vassar College. She earned a doctorate in math from Yale University in 1934.

BORN: December 9, 1906, in New York City, New York

DIED: January 1, 1992

EDUCATION: Vassar College, Yale University

KNOWN FOR: developed the COBOL programming language

JOINING THE NAVY

In the 1940s, the U.S. entered World War II. Hopper wanted to help. She joined the U.S. Naval Reserve in 1943. She was assigned to work on the Mark I, a computer used to do calculations to help the war effort. Hopper wrote the first-ever computer manual in 1946.

A NEW LANGUAGE

After the war, Hopper continued working with computers. In 1949, she began working on the UNIVAC. It was the first commercial computer made in the U.S. Hopper's work led to the development of a computer language called COBOL in 1959. By the 1970s, COBOL was used on computers around the world.

A LONG CAREER

Hopper retired from the Navy in 1966. But she soon returned to work on programming languages. She retired again in 1986 after being promoted to rear admiral. Her work on programming languages made her a computer pioneer.

AWARDS AND HONORS

- **1991** National Medal of Technology and Innovation
- **1994** National Women's Hall of Fame
- **2016** Presidential Medal of Freedom

TIMELINE

- **1934** earns a doctorate in math
- **1944** begins working on the Mark I
- **1949** begins working on UNIVAC
- **1959** the COBOL programming language is developed
- **1986** retires from the Navy

Linus Torvalds

Linus Torvalds is a computer scientist from Finland who developed Linux. It is the basis for much of today's internet!

TIMELINE

1991 releases the first version of Linux

1996 earns a master's degree in computer science from the University of Helsinki

1999 IBM begins support for Linux

2005 releases Git

2011 releases Subsurface, a software for scuba divers

AN EARLY INTEREST

Torvalds became interested in computers at a young age. He learned on his grandfather's Commodore VIC-20 computer. He began studying computer science at the University of Helsinki in 1988.

A NEW IDEA

In college, Torvalds used a computer with the MS-DOS **operating system** (OS). But he wanted to create a new OS based on UNIX. UNIX is made up of different parts that can be fit together and used in different ways. In 1991, Torvalds finished his project. He called it Linux. It was free for others to use and change.

LINUX TAKES OVER

Use of Linux spread quickly. It was used on personal computers, supercomputers, and more. By the late 1990s, large computer companies such as IBM began supporting Linux. Today, Linux is used across the internet. The Android mobile OS is based on Linux. Amazon Web Services and Google Cloud Platform also use Linux. Torvalds continues to work on Linux as its lead developer.

TUX

Since 1996, Linux's mascot has been a penguin character named Tux.

BEYOND LINUX

In 2005, Torvalds created the **open-source** program Git. This important tool makes it easy for programmers to collaborate and track changes to their work over time. The internet would not be what it is today without Torvalds's innovations.

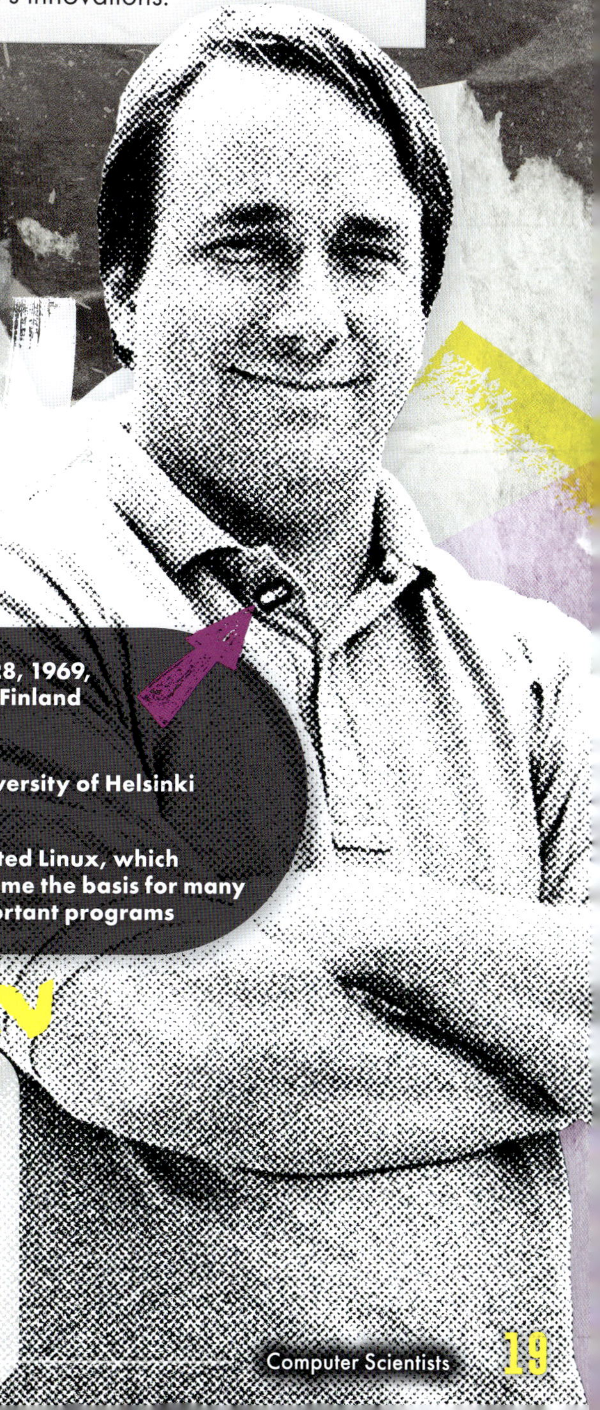

BORN: December 28, 1969, in Helsinki, Finland

EDUCATION: University of Helsinki

KNOWN FOR: created Linux, which became the basis for many important programs

AWARDS AND HONORS

- **2012** Millennium Technology Prize
- **2012** Internet Hall of Fame
- **2014** IEEE Computer Society Computer Pioneer Award

PHYSICISTS

Albert Einstein is one of the best-known scientists and thinkers of all time. His work has shaped the way people understand the universe and how it works.

Albert Einstein

EARLY LIFE

Einstein was a curious child. He was fascinated by a compass his father gave him and wanted to learn how it worked. In 1896, he began studying at the Federal Polytechnic School in Switzerland. After graduating, he got a job at the Swiss Patent Office. In his spare time, he did scientific research.

THE MIRACLE YEAR

In 1905, Einstein's research paid off. He published four groundbreaking papers. He wrote about light, atoms, and the relationship between space and time. The final paper included the famous equation $E=mc^2$, which explains the relationship between energy and mass.

FIRST PAPER

Einstein wrote his first scientific paper at age 16. It was about the magnets that made his compass work.

FINDING FAME

In time, Einstein's papers drew attention. He began traveling the world giving lectures. Einstein also continued his research. In 1915, he introduced the theory of general relativity in a paper. This theory explains how gravity works.

LIFE IN THE UNITED STATES

In the 1930s, the Nazi movement was on the rise in Europe. Nazi leaders targeted Einstein's career and rights because he was Jewish. He left Germany, eventually moving to the U.S. to teach in 1933. There, Einstein worked on combining all of the forces of physics into one theory. He called it unified field theory. He continued this work until his death in 1955. Today's scientists continue work on this theory.

BORN: March 14, 1879, in Ulm, Germany

DIED: April 18, 1955

EDUCATION: Federal Polytechnic School

KNOWN FOR: developed theories to explain the relationship between space, time, energy, and mass

AWARDS AND HONORS

- 1921 Nobel Prize in Physics
- 1925 Copley Medal
- 1929 Max Planck Medal

"The important thing is to not stop questioning. Curiosity has its own reason for existence."
— Albert Einstein

TIMELINE

1896 begins attending Federal Polytechnic School

1905 publishes four groundbreaking physics papers

1912 begins teaching at the Federal Polytechnic School

1915 introduces the theory of general relativity

1933 moves to the U.S.

Stephen Hawking

Stephen Hawking is one of the world's most famous physicists. He helped explain the relationship between space and time in a way ordinary people could understand.

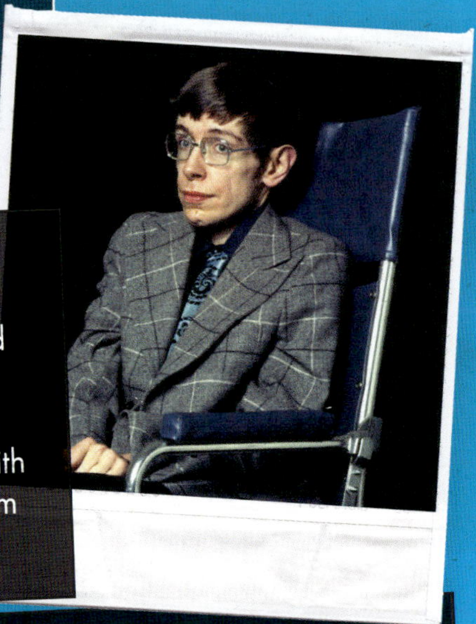

EARLY LIFE

Hawking was interested in space growing up. He gained entrance to the University of Oxford in 1959. There, he studied physics. He attended the University of Cambridge for his doctorate. While there, Hawking was diagnosed with amyotrophic lateral sclerosis (ALS). The disease caused him to slowly lose control of his muscles.

EXPLORING BLACK HOLES

ALS did not slow Hawking down. He earned his doctorate in 1966. Much of his research focused on black holes. In 1974, he theorized that black holes can give off radiation in certain conditions. This phenomenon was named "Hawking radiation." In 1977, he became a professor at Cambridge.

SCIENCE CELEBRITY

In the 1980s, Hawking began focusing on how the universe formed. In 1988, he published *A Brief History of Time*. This book used simple language to explain the history of the universe. It sold more than 10 million copies. Hawking traveled the world giving lectures and making TV appearances.

WRITING FOR CHILDREN

In 2007, Hawking and his daughter Lucy cowrote a children's book called *George's Secret Key to the Universe*.

TIMELINE

1962 earns a degree in physics from Oxford

1963 is diagnosed with ALS

1966 earns a doctorate from Cambridge

BORN: January 8, 1942, in Oxford, England

DIED: March 14, 2018

EDUCATION: University of Oxford, University of Cambridge

KNOWN FOR: researched black holes and the history of the universe

FINAL THOUGHTS

Hawking continued his work until his death in 2018. His final paper was published a few months after he died. Hawking is remembered as one of the greatest thinkers of modern times.

AWARDS AND HONORS

- **1974** Royal Society
- **2006** Copley Medal
- **2009** Presidential Medal of Freedom

1974 publishes research showing black holes give off radiation

1988 publishes *A Brief History of Time*

2018 final paper is published

Luis Alvarez was a physicist who invented new ways to detect and study **subatomic particles**. His work led to the creation of the atomic bomb.

Luis Alvarez

EXPLORING RADIOACTIVITY

When he was young, Alvarez was fascinated by science. He went on to study physics at the University of Chicago. He earned his doctorate there in 1936. In 1938, he discovered that the atoms of certain radioactive elements decay by combining an electron with a **nucleus**, creating a new type of element.

MILITARY WORK

In 1940, Alvarez began working at the Massachusetts Institute of Technology (MIT). There, he developed radar systems that helped the military locate targets. Starting in 1943, Alvarez worked on the Manhattan Project to help develop the first atomic bomb. In 1945, he became a professor of physics at the University of California, Berkeley.

PRIZE-WINNING WORK

In the 1950s, Alvarez introduced his idea for a liquid hydrogen **bubble chamber**. The device would use liquid hydrogen to help discover new particles and study their behavior. The device led to the discovery of many previously unknown particles. Alvarez won a Nobel Prize for this work in 1968.

OTHER DISCOVERIES

In 1980, Alvarez and his son Walter found evidence of a large asteroid strike on Earth around 65 million years ago. They believed its impact caused the sudden extinction of dinosaurs, a theory accepted by many today.

BORN: June 13, 1911, in San Francisco, California

DIED: September 1, 1988

EDUCATION: University of Chicago

KNOWN FOR: discovered how radioactive elements decay and created the bubble chamber

SAN FRANCISCO

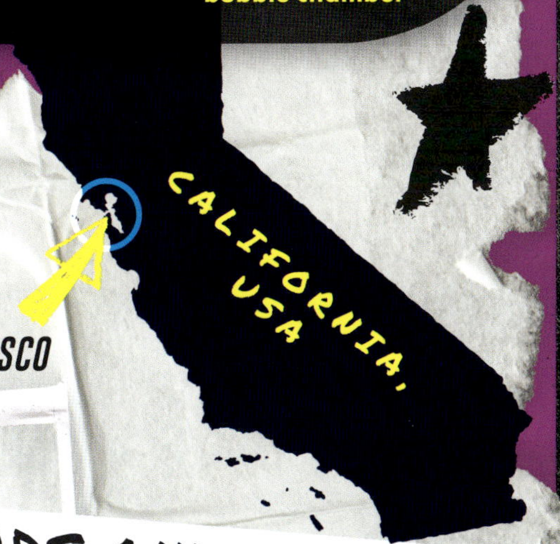

AWARDS AND HONORS

- 1963 National Medal of Science
- 1968 Nobel Prize in Physics
- 1987 Enrico Fermi Award

FREQUENT FLYER

Alvarez loved aviation almost as much as he loved science. He learned to pilot airplanes in 1934 and continued flying for the next 50 years.

TIMELINE

1936 earns a doctorate from the University of Chicago

1940 begins working at MIT

1943 begins working on the Manhattan Project

1950s introduces the liquid hydrogen bubble chamber

1980 develops a theory about an asteroid causing the extinction of dinosaurs

Peter Higgs

Peter Higgs was a physicist who is credited with unlocking some of the universe's deepest secrets. He proposed the existence of a subatomic particle that gives mass to other particles. In 2012, the particle was discovered!

MATH AND SCIENCE

As a child, Higgs won chemistry prizes in school. He went on to study physics at the University of London. He earned a doctorate in 1954.

MYSTERIOUS MASS

In 1964, Higgs wrote a paper proposing that an invisible energy field exists across the universe. He theorized that particles interact with this field to receive mass. The theory was later called the Higgs mechanism.

HEAVY BOSONS

Later that year, Higgs revised his paper. He included a theory about a type of particle called a heavy boson. Higgs theorized that this particle existed within the Higgs mechanism to give other particles mass. In time, it became known as the Higgs boson. But physicists could not yet prove its existence.

TIMELINE

1954 earns a doctorate in physics from King's College, University of London

1960 begins teaching mathematical physics at the University of Edinburgh

BORN: May 29, 1929, in Newcastle upon Tyne, England

DIED: April 8, 2024

EDUCATION: King's College, University of London

KNOWN FOR: discovered the Higgs boson

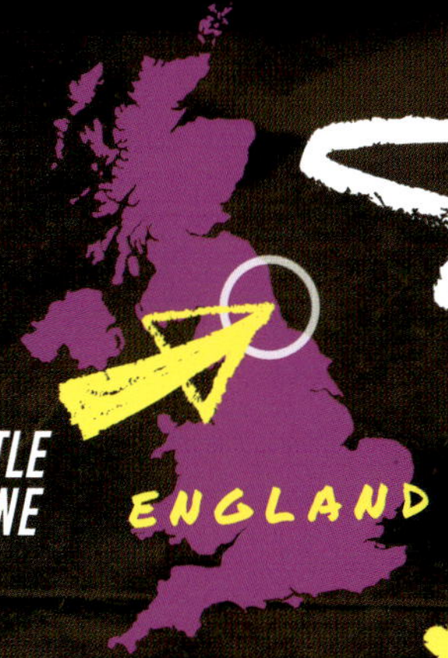

AWARDS AND HONORS

- **1983** Royal Society fellow
- **2013** Nobel Prize in Physics
- **2015** Copley Medal

PROVING A THEORY

In 2012, after nearly 50 years of research, the Higgs boson was finally discovered! Scientists used a machine called the Large Hadron Collider (LHC) to detect it. The next year, Higgs won the Nobel Prize in Physics for his work with the Higgs boson. Higgs died in 2024. His work continues to influence the work of other physicists.

- **1964** publishes theories about the Higgs mechanism and the Higgs boson
- **2012** the existence of the Higgs boson is confirmed
- **2013** wins the Nobel Prize in Physics

EARTH AND CLIMATE SCIENTISTS

Marcia McNutt is a geophysicist who has helped scientists better understand the ocean floor. She took part in 15 major ocean expeditions, leading many as chief scientist.

A PASSION FOR LEARNING

McNutt graduated at the top of her class in high school. She went on to study physics at Colorado College, where she earned a bachelor's degree in 1973. She earned her doctorate in earth sciences in 1978. She researched why volcanoes are active in the middle of **tectonic plates**.

UNDERSEA SCIENCE

In 1982, McNutt began working at MIT. She focused her research on an unusually shallow part of the South Pacific Ocean called a superswell. In 1990, she published an important paper exploring the superswell. The paper inspired further scientific research. In 1997, McNutt became president of the Monterey Bay Aquarium Research Institute (MBARI) in California. There, she continued research on how volcanoes affect Earth's **lithosphere**.

OIL SPILL

In 2009, McNutt became the first woman to lead the U.S. Geological Survey (USGS). The next year, an oil rig called *Deepwater Horizon* exploded. It spilled millions of gallons of oil into the Gulf of Mexico. McNutt led a team of scientists tasked with investigating the spill. She was praised for her leadership during this time.

BREAKING BARRIERS

In 2013, McNutt left the USGS to become the first female editor-in-chief of *Science* magazine. She continues to be a leader in earth science and oceanography!

AWARDS AND HONORS

- **1988** James B. Macelwane Medal
- **2007** Maurice Ewing Medal
- **2022** AAG Atlas Award

BORN: February 19, 1952, in Minneapolis, Minnesota

EDUCATION: Colorado College, Scripps Institution of Oceanography

KNOWN FOR: researched superswells and underwater volcanoes and helped manage the *Deepwater Horizon* oil spill

MINNEAPOLIS

UNDERWATER RESEARCH

While working at MBARI, McNutt oversaw the building of the first deep-sea cabled observatory in U.S. waters!

TIMELINE

1990 publishes a paper about a superswell in the South Pacific Ocean

2009 becomes the first woman to direct the USGS

2010 guides the U.S. response to the *Deepwater Horizon* oil spill

2013 becomes the first female editor-in-chief of *Science* magazine

2016 becomes the first female president of the National Academy of Sciences

Susan Solomon

Susan Solomon is an atmospheric scientist who made important discoveries about air pollution and Earth's ozone layer. She is famous for leading research about **climate change**.

SCIENCE WHIZ

Solomon grew up with an interest in science. In high school, she won third place at a national science fair. She went on to study chemistry in college. In 1981, Solomon earned a doctorate in chemistry from the University of California, Berkeley. She soon began working for the National Oceanic and Atmospheric Administration (NOAA).

A HOLE IN THE OZONE

In the 1980s, many scientists became concerned with a hole in the ozone above Antarctica. Solomon suspected the ozone hole was caused by pollutants called chlorofluorocarbons (CFCs). She theorized that when CFCs combined with certain conditions in the clouds above Antarctica, the ozone hole grew. In the 1980s, Solomon led expeditions to Antarctica. She took measurements that proved her theory was correct.

NEW LAWS

CFCs were commonly found in refrigerators, cleaning chemicals, and many other household objects. In 1990, the Montreal Protocol banned the use of CFCs by the year 2010. Thanks to Solomon's work, the hole in the ozone continues to shrink today.

TIMELINE

1981 earns a doctorate in chemistry

1986 leads the first expedition to Antarctica to study the hole in the ozone layer

AWARDS AND HONORS

- **1999** National Medal of Science
- **2004** Blue Planet Prize
- **2018** Crafoord Prize in Geosciences

BORN: January 19, 1956, in Chicago, Illinois

EDUCATION: Illinois Institute of Technology; University of California, Berkeley

KNOWN FOR: proved that CFCs caused the ozone hole and led research on climate change

MORE CLIMATE LEADERSHIP

In 2002, Solomon joined the Intergovernmental Panel on Climate Change (IPCC). Under Solomon's leadership, the IPCC confirmed that climate change is caused by humans. In 2007, the IPCC won the Nobel Peace Prize for this work. Solomon continues to study atmospheric science at MIT.

- **1990** the Montreal Protocol bans the use of CFCs by 2010
- **2002** joins the IPCC to research the impact of climate change
- **2012** begins working at MIT

Syukuro Manabe

Syukuro Manabe is a meteorologist known for his research on Earth's atmosphere and climate. His work has helped people understand the threat of climate change.

WATCHING THE WEATHER

From a young age, Manabe was fascinated by weather. He went on to study meteorology at the University of Tokyo. After earning his doctorate in 1958, Manabe moved to the U.S. to work for the U.S. Weather Bureau, now called the National Weather Service (NWS).

MAKING A MODEL

Manabe joined the Geophysical Fluid Dynamics Laboratory in 1963. He studied how Earth's atmosphere affected weather patterns. In 1967, he created the first reliable 3D climate model of the atmosphere. The model showed how **greenhouse gases** raise global temperatures.

CARBON AND CLIMATE

Carbon dioxide is one of the most common greenhouse gases. It is commonly released into the atmosphere through farming and when **fossil fuels** are burned. In 1975, Manabe used his model to show the impact of carbon dioxide on Earth's climate. He predicted Earth's climate would continue to warm as more carbon dioxide was released into the atmosphere.

WARMING WORLD ★

Earth's average temperature has risen about about 2 degrees Fahrenheit (1.1 degrees Celsius) since 1850.

LATER LIFE

In 2005, Manabe became Princeton University's senior meteorologist. In 2020, he cowrote the book *Beyond Global Warming*. It details how scientists used computers and models to discover climate change. In 2021, Manabe won the Nobel Prize in Physics for his contributions to physical climate modeling.

BORN: September 21, 1931, in Shingū, Japan

EDUCATION: University of Tokyo

KNOWN FOR: created the first reliable climate model and helped spread knowledge about climate change

AWARDS AND HONORS

- **1992** Blue Planet Prize
- **2018** Crafoord Prize in Geosciences
- **2021** Nobel Prize in Physics

TIMELINE

- **1958** earns a doctorate in meteorology from the University of Tokyo
- **1967** creates a groundbreaking 3D model of Earth's atmosphere
- **1975** uses his model to show the impacts of carbon dioxide on Earth's atmosphere
- **2005** becomes senior meteorologist at Princeton University
- **2020** cowrites the book *Beyond Global Warming*

ASTRONOMERS

Carl Sagan is an astronomer known for his ability to communicate scientific ideas to the public. His research on the planets and his curiosity about extraterrestrial intelligence paved the way for scientists to continue the search for life beyond Earth.

YOUNG ASTRONOMER

Young Sagan read science-fiction stories and dreamed about life on other planets. At 16, he began studying physics, astronomy, and astrophysics at the University of Chicago. Sagan earned a doctorate in 1960 and began researching the atmospheres of Venus and other planets.

Carl Sagan

BORN: November 9, 1934, in New York City, New York

DIED: December 20, 1996

EDUCATION: University of Chicago

KNOWN FOR: researched planets and paved the way for study of life beyond Earth

STUDYING THE SOLAR SYSTEM

In 1968, Sagan became director of Cornell University's Laboratory for Planetary Studies. Around this time, he also helped plan missions for NASA space probes. His study of other planets continued. He researched the seasons of Mars. He even uncovered why one of Saturn's moons is yellow. When the *Voyager* space probes launched in 1977, Sagan included a message intended for other life-forms that could discover the probes one day.

SCIENCE CELEBRITY

Sagan shared his passion for science with the public. His 1977 book *The Dragons of Eden* won a Pulitzer Prize. In 1980, he and his wife, Ann Druyan, created the TV series *Cosmos*. This popular show explores astronomy concepts. Sagan continued to use his celebrity to advance astronomy until his death in 1996. His work has changed the way many scientists relate to the public.

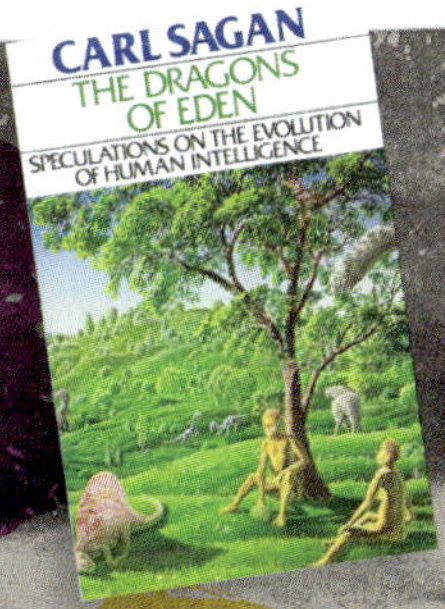

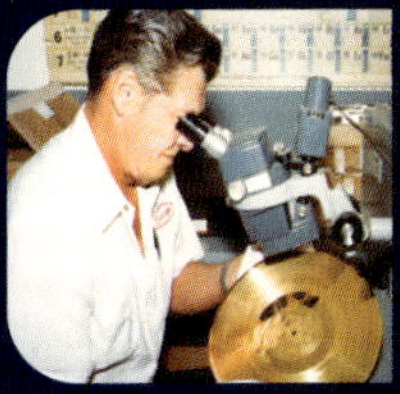

SIGHTS AND SOUNDS

The *Voyager* probes included a record featuring photos of life on Earth and recordings of music and animal sounds.

AWARDS AND HONORS

1977, 1981
NASA Distinguished Public Service Medal

1978
Pulitzer Prize in Nonfiction

1994
National Academy of Sciences Public Welfare Medal

TIMELINE

1960
earns a doctorate in astronomy and astrophysics

1968
becomes the director of Cornell University's Laboratory for Planetary Studies

1977
helps craft a message included on the *Voyager* space probes

1980
cofounds the Planetary Society, an international organization focused on space exploration

SEPTEMBER 1980
writes and hosts the TV series *Cosmos*

Carolyn Porco

Carolyn Porco is a planetary scientist known for her work exploring the outer solar system. She has helped take never-before-seen pictures of Saturn and its rings. Her research has given scientists a better understanding of the outer planets.

SEEING SATURN

At age 13, Porco first spotted Saturn through a friend's telescope. She dreamed of studying the planet one day. She went on to study science at Stony Brook University, graduating in 1974.

VOYAGER

In 1983, Porco earned a doctorate in planetary science. That same year, she joined the team studying images taken by the *Voyager* space probes. She discovered a connection between Saturn's rings and its magnetic field.

FAMOUS PHOTO

One of Porco's most famous images is called *The Day the Earth Smiled*. It shows Saturn's rings as well as Earth and the moon as tiny dots.

AWARDS AND HONORS

- **2008** Isaac Asimov Science Award
- **2010** Carl Sagan Medal
- **2020** Sikkens Prize

TIMELINE

- **1983** earns a doctorate in planetary science
- **1990** is appointed to lead the imaging team of the *Cassini* mission

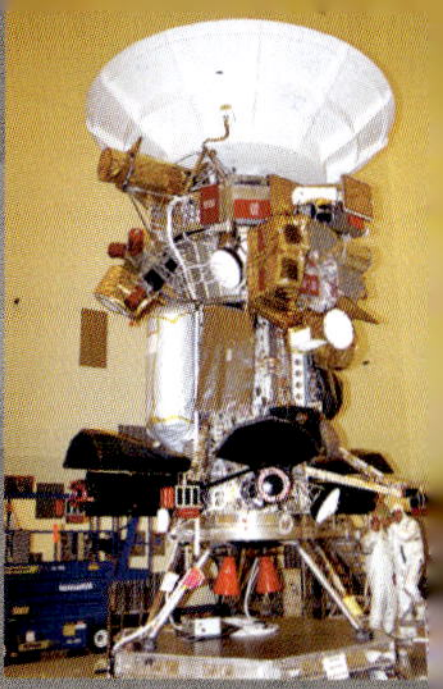

CASSINI

In 1990, Porco was chosen to lead the imaging team for the *Cassini* mission. Her team created instruments that let the space probe take high-quality photos of planets. *Cassini* arrived at Saturn in 2004. It took incredible color photos. It also helped make many discoveries, including seven new moons of Saturn and an ocean on the moon Enceladus.

SHARING SCIENCE

The *Cassini* mission ended in 2017. Porco continues to publish papers and give talks about her research. In 2017, she was the guest editor for an issue of *Astrobiology* about Enceladus. She continues to share her passion for astronomy and faraway planets.

BORN: March 6, 1953, in New York City, New York

EDUCATION: Stony Brook University, California Institute of Technology

KNOWN FOR: led imaging team on *Cassini* mission, ensuring detailed photos of Saturn

2004 *Cassini* reaches Saturn after nearly seven years of travel

2013 helps take *The Day the Earth Smiled*, a photo of Earth as seen from Saturn

2017 guest edits an issue of *Astrobiology* magazine

BIOLOGISTS

Charles Darwin was a biologist best known for developing the theories of **evolution** and **natural selection**. He is one of the most influential scientists in history.

A LOVE OF NATURE

Darwin grew up in a wealthy family. His father was a doctor, and his grandfather was a **botanist**. From a young age, Darwin loved exploring nature. At 16, he began studying medicine. But he soon switched his focus to natural history.

SAILING ON THE BEAGLE

Starting in 1831, Darwin took part in a five-year mission to sail around the world on the HMS *Beagle*. He joined the mission as a naturalist. He collected samples of plants, animals, and fossils. In the Galápagos Islands, Darwin noticed that some birds looked similar to birds found in other places. But they had **adaptations** that helped them live in the Galápagos Islands. This formed the basis of his future work.

A NEW THEORY

Darwin spent years studying the samples he had collected. He developed a new theory. He believed all living things had evolved to their current form over a long period of time through a process called natural selection. In 1859, Darwin published a book about his theory called *On the Origin of Species by Means of Natural Selection*. Many still accept Darwin's theory today.

LATER LIFE

Darwin's later research focused on animal emotions and the movements of plants. His ideas changed the ways in which people viewed the natural world.

AWARDS AND HONORS

- 1853 Royal Medal
- 1864 Copley Medal
- 1879 Baly Medal

BORN: February 12, 1809, in Shrewsbury, England

DIED: April 19, 1882

EDUCATION: University of Edinburgh, University of Cambridge

KNOWN FOR: developed the theory of evolution through natural selection

TIMELINE

- **1825** begins studying medicine at the University of Edinburgh
- **1831** finishes studying at the University of Cambridge and begins his journey around the world
- **1836** returns to England to study samples from his journey
- **1839** publishes a research journal containing notes from his travels
- **1859** publishes *On the Origin of Species by Means of Natural Selection*

Sylvia Earle

Sylvia Earle is an oceanographer and marine biologist. Her work has helped draw attention to ocean pollution and **conservation**.

EARLY LIFE

When she was young, Earle's family moved to Florida. There, Earle fell in love with exploring the ocean. She studied botany in college. She also learned to SCUBA dive. This allowed her to study the ocean environment up close.

OCEAN EXPLORER

In 1966, Earle earned a doctorate from Duke University. She focused her research on ocean algae. Meanwhile, Earle took part in ocean expeditions worldwide. She was one of the first scientists to use SCUBA to study marine life up close. In 1968, Earle discovered two new undersea dunes off the coast of the Bahamas.

GIBBSTOWN

BORN: August 30, 1935, in Gibbstown, New Jersey

EDUCATION: Florida State University, Duke University

KNOWN FOR: participated in many expeditions to study the ocean and bring awareness to ocean pollution

TIMELINE

1966 earns a doctorate

1968 discovers new undersea dunes near the Bahamas

1970 leads a team of scientists in a two-week experiment in an underwater habitat

1977 becomes the first woman to serve as chief scientist of NOAA

2009 helps found Mission Blue

DIVING DEEP

In 1970, Earle led a team of scientists who spent two weeks living 50 feet (15.2 meters) underwater. The Tektite II experiment studied the health effects of underwater living. The expedition made Earle a celebrity!

SAVING THE SEA

During the Tektite II experiment, Earle observed how pollution affected the ocean. She set out to conserve oceans and ocean life. In 1980, she starred in a documentary that called for the protection of sperm whales.

OTHER WORK

In 1990, Earle was named the chief scientist of NOAA. She helped advise the U.S. government on ocean and climate policies. In 2009, Earle helped found Mission Blue. This organization is dedicated to protecting marine habitats worldwide.

AWARDS AND HONORS

- **1998** — ***TIME* Hero for the Planet**
- **2009** — **TED Prize**
- **2014** — **Champions of the Earth Lifetime Achievement Award**

> "If you've never touched the ocean, the ocean touches you with every breath you take."
> —Sylvia Earle

Tu Youyou is a Chinese pharmacologist known for combining modern medicine with ancient Chinese practices. Her work led to a cure for malaria.

Tu Youyou

STUDYING SCIENCE

When Tu was a teenager, she became very sick. She decided to pursue a career in medicine so she could help other sick people. In 1951, she began attending Beijing Medical College. She studied both traditional Chinese medicine and Western medicine. She learned how to use pharmaceutical science to develop medicines.

SEARCHING FOR A CURE

In 1969, Tu was appointed to lead a team developing a cure for malaria. This disease infects the bloodstream through mosquito bites. Tu researched ancient Chinese treatments. She studied hundreds of plants that might hold cures. She then used modern medical practices to test parts from the plants. In 1972, Tu's team discovered a compound from the *qinghao* plant could be used to destroy the **parasites** that cause malaria. The deadly disease finally had a cure!

DEADLY DISEASE

Malaria is carried by mosquitoes in tropical and subtropical climates. The disease kills about 600,000 people per year, making it one of the greatest threats to public health.

TIMELINE

1962 completes her medical training

1969 begins leading a team in the search for a malaria cure

CONTINUING RESEARCH

In 1981, Tu presented her findings to the world. In 2001, the World Health Organization (WHO) began recommending malaria treatments based on Tu's compound, now known as artemisinin. In 2015, Tu won the Nobel Prize in Physiology or Medicine. Her work has saved millions of lives!

AWARDS AND HONORS

- **2011** Lasker-DeBakey Clinical Medical Research Award
- **2015** Nobel Prize in Physiology or Medicine
- **2019** Chinese government's Medal of the Republic

BORN: December 30, 1930, in Ningbo, China

EDUCATION: Beijing Medical College, Academy of Traditional Chinese Medicine

KNOWN FOR: developed a treatment for malaria

1972 discovers that a compound from the *qinghao* plant can treat malaria

1981 presents her findings to the world for the first time

2015 wins a Nobel Prize for artemisinin

THE FUTURE OF SCIENCE

From biology to physics to astronomy, scientists have helped humans make sense of the world around us. Their work improves our lives with new technologies and medicines. They explore the farthest reaches of space and the deepest parts of the ocean. Scientists are always pushing human knowledge forward, with new discoveries happening every day.

MORE SCIENTISTS TODAY AND BEYOND

CHRISTOPHER JACKSON

Christopher Jackson is a geologist and science communicator. His work focuses on how geological processes affect sedimentary basins. These are areas of Earth's crust that have thick layers of sedimentary rock. Jackson used a process called seismic reflection to study the rock. He won the 2013 Bigsby Medal for his work.

KATE MARVEL

Kate Marvel is a climate scientist who specializes in climate modeling. She studies how Earth's temperature and climate might change in the future. Marvel is also a well-known science writer who frequently appears on podcasts.

NIZAR IBRAHIM

Nizar Ibrahim is a paleontologist who studies fossils from the Cretaceous period, which ended around 66 million years ago. Ibrahim has discovered fossilized footprints and dinosaur bones that provide clues about what life was like during this era.

LUCIANNE WALKOWICZ

Lucianne Walkowicz is an astronomer. They study planets that could support human life. Walkowicz also works to promote social justice in astronomy and other scientific fields.

JEDIDAH ISLER

Jedidah Isler is an astrophysicist and educator whose work centers on using science to advance social justice. She studied black holes before focusing on science policy. Isler works to promote more diversity in scientific fields.

RONA CHANDRAWATI

Rona Chandrawati is a bioengineer. She studies how **nanotechnology** could be used to detect contaminated food. She is also a professor at the University of New South Wales in Australia.

GLOSSARY

adaptations—changes an animal or plant undergoes over a long period of time to fit where it lives

artificial intelligence—a computer's ability to do things a human mind can do

biotechnology—the use of biological processes to produce products, especially medicines

botanist—a person who studies plants

bubble chamber—a device used to find and track the paths of subatomic particles

climate change—a human-caused change in Earth's weather due to warming temperatures

conservation—the careful protection of something

DNA—material that carries information about the makeup of a living thing

evolution—the process through which organisms change over time to adapt to their environment

fermentation—the breakdown of a substance caused by bacteria or other microorganisms

fossil fuels—fuels such as coal, oil, and natural gas that were formed in the earth from plant or animal remains

greenhouse gases—gases that trap heat in Earth's atmosphere and lead to climate change; greenhouse gases include carbon dioxide and chlorofluorocarbons.

lithosphere—the hard outer layer of the earth

metamorphosis—the change from one stage to the next

microorganisms—life-forms that are too small to be seen without a microscope, such as bacteria, protozoa, fungi, and viruses

nanotechnology—the study of matter at a very small scale; nanotechnology is used to create new materials and devices.

natural selection—a process in which the organisms with physical traits best suited to a particular environment are more likely to survive, passing those traits on to their descendants

nucleus—the central part of an atom that contains nearly all of its mass

open-source—related to software that is freely available to be distributed and modified

operating system—computer software that allows programs to run

pandemic—a widespread disease outbreak that affects many people

parasites—living things that survive on or in other living things; parasites offer nothing for the food and protection they receive.

radiation—energy given off in the form of waves

RNA—material that carries instructions to make proteins

subatomic particles—particles smaller than an atom

tectonic plates—parts of Earth's crust that move

X-ray diffraction—the use of X-rays to determine the structure of an object

WRITE ABOUT IT!

- What scientific topics do you want to learn more about? **Why do they interest you?**
- Which scientists inspire you? **Why?**
- Have you ever done a scientific experiment? **If so, what did you learn from it?**

ALSO CHECK OUT

INDEX

The images in this book are reproduced through the courtesy of: Bengt Nyman/ Wikimedia Commons, front cover (Youyou), pp. 26 (Higgs top), 33 (Manabe profile), 43 (Youyou profile); Christopher Michel/ Wikimedia Commons, front cover (Karikó), pp. 28 (McNutt top), 29 (McNutt profile); Ferdinand Schmutzer/ Wikimedia Commons, front cover (Einstein); Mickey Adair/ Getty Images, p. 3 (Sagan); Cavan Images/ Alamy Stock Photo, pp. 3 (Solomon), 31 (Solomon main, Solomon profile); Paul Ehrenfest/ Wikimedia Commons, pp. 3 (Einstein), 20-21; LILLIAN SUWANRUMPHA/ Getty Images, p. 4-5 (main photo); Stebunik/ Wikimedia Commons, p. 5 (1796); Julius Jääskeläinen/ Wikimedia Commons, pp. 5 (1859), 38 (Darwin main); National Science Foundation/ Wikimedia Commons, p. 5 (1950s); vitstudio, p. 5 (1990); NASA/ Johns Hopkins APL/ Steve Gribben/ Wikimedia Commons, p. 5 (2024); Allistair/ peopleimages.com, p. 6 (chemist); goodluz, p. 6 (biologist); Mr. Grey/ Wikimedia Commons, p. 7 (Anning); RDB/ ullstein/ Getty Images, p. 7 (Piaget); GlaxoSmithKline plc/ Wikimedia Commons, p. 7 (Elion); Geschenk von Louise Bachofen-Burckhardt 1904/ Wikimedia Commons, p. 7 (Merian); Jarould/ Wikimedia Commons, p. 8 (Curie top); Scewing/ Wikimedia Commons, p. 8 (Curie main); Wellcome Collection/ Wikimedia Commons, pp. 9 (Curie top), 10 (Pasteur main); VictoriaKC/ Wikimedia Commons, p. 9 (Curie profile); Agence de presse Meurisse/ Wikimedia Commons, p. 9 (Irene Curie); MKavalenkau, p. 9 (Warsaw); Benjamin R. Tucker/ Wikimedia Commons, p. 10 (Pasteur top); Felix Nadar/ Wikimedia Commons, p. 11 (Pasteur top); maitrecortex, p. 11 (Dole); Ondra Havala/ Wikimedia Commons, p. 11 (Pasteur left); Nadar/ Wikimedia Commons, p. 11 (Pasteur profile); Raymond Gosling/ Wikimedia Commons, p. 12 (photo 51); Photocreo Bednarek, p. 12 (London); Photo 12/ Getty Images, p. 13 (Franklin main); MRC Laboratory of Molecular Biology/ Wikimedia Commons, p. 13 (Franklin profile); Szegedi Tudományegyetem/ Wikimedia Commons, p. 14 (Karikó top); Taylor Hill/ Getty Images, p. 14 (Karikó main); Ignácz Csaba/ Wikimedia Commons, p. 15 (Kisújszállás); Stefania D'Alessandro/ Getty Images, p. 15 (Karikó profile); Seregadushka/ Wikimedia Commons, p. 16 (Hopper top); The U.S. National Archives/ nara.getarchive, pp. 16 (Hopper main), 24-25 (Alvarez main), 25 (Alvarez); National Archives at College Park - Still Pictures/ Wikimedia Commons, p. 16 (Hopper profile); Tierney, p. 16 (New York City); Jan Arkesteijn/ Wikimedia Commons, p. 17; pixabay/ Wikimedia Commons, p. 18 (Tux); Krd/ Wikimedia Commons, p. 19 (Torvalds top); Scanrail, p. 19 (Helsinki); Jarno Mela/ AFP/ Getty Images, p. 19 (Torvalds profile); Martin Streicher/ Wikimedia Commons, p. 19 (Torvalds main); Orren Jack Turner/ Wikimedia Commons, p. 21 (Einstein profile); EdVal, p. 21 (Ulm); NASA/ Wikimedia Commons, p. 22 (Hawking top); John Hedgecoe/ Popperfoto/ Getty Images, p. 22 (Stephen Hawking middle); GrahamHardy/ Wikimedia Commons, p. 22 (book); Jim Campbell/ Aero-News Network/ Wikimedia Commons, p. 23 (Hawking profile); greir, p. 23 (Oxford); Brian Randle/ Mirrorpix/ Getty Images, p. 23 (Stephen Hawking main); Lawrence Berkeley National Laboratory/ Department of Energy/ Wikimedia Commons, p. 25 (Alvarez profile); ByDroneVideos, p. 25 (San Francisco); Peter Macdiarmid/ Getty Images, p. 26 (Higgs); Leonardo Cendamo/ Getty Images, pp. 26-27 (Higgs main); Hans G/ Wikimedia Commons, p. 27 (Higgs profile); Elizabeth, p. 27 (Newcastle upon Tyne); Jesse Grant/ Getty Images, p. 28 (McNutt main); stevengaertner, p. 29 (Minneapolis); Conrad Erb/ Wikimedia Commons, p. 30 (Solomon); Iuliia Sokolovska, p. 31 (Chicago); KENA BETANCUR/ Getty Images, p. 32 (Manabe main); 663highland/ Wikimedia Commons, p. 33 (Shingu); Mark Makela/ Getty Images, p. 33 (Manabe bottom); Mickey Adair/ Michael Ochs Archives/ Getty Images, p. 34 (Sagan main); James M. Kelly/ Alamy Stock Photo, p. 34 (Sagan profile); Taiga, p. 34 (New York City); Melesse/ Wikipedia, p. 35 (Dragons of Eden); NASA/ JPL/ Wikimedia Commons, p. 35 (Sights and Sounds, Sagan bottom); Stephen Shugerman/ Getty Images, p. 36 (Porco main); Sgerbic/ Wikimedia Commons, p. 36 (Porco top); NASA/ JPL/ SSI/ CICLOPS/ Wikimedia Commons, p. 36 (famous photo); National Aeronautics and Space Administration/ Wikimedia Commons, p. 37 (top photo); Giuseppe Cammino, p. 37 (New York City); Christopher Michel/ Wikimedia Commons, p. 37 (Porco profile); John Collier/ Wikimedia Commons, p. 38 (Darwin top); Elliott & Fry/ Wikimedia Commons, p. 39 (Darwin profile); Richard Hayman, p. 39 (Shrewsbury); Joseph Echteler/ Wikimedia Commons, p. 39 (sculpture); Mr. Matté/ Wikimedia Commons, p. 40 (Gibbstown); Steve Jurvetson/ Wikimedia Commons, p. 40 (Earle profile); USFWS Pacific/ Wikimedia Commons, p. 41 (Earle top); Gisela Schober/ Getty Images, p. 41 (Earle main); Xinhua News Agency/ Getty Images, p. 42 (Youyou main); SupapleX/ Wikimedia Commons, p. 42 (top photo); Xinhua/ Yang Wumin/ Getty Images, p. 43 (Youyou Top photo); Weiming, p. 43 (Ningbo); John Gaffen/ Alamy Stock Photo, p. 44 (Jackson); Norwegian University of Science and Technology/ Wikimedia Commons, p. 44 (Marvel); Bill O'Leary/ Getty Images, p. 45 (Ibrahim); Vacationpaste/ Wikimedia Commons, p. 45 (Walkowicz); Jemal Countess/ Getty Images, p. 45 (Isler); Meng Chenguang/ Xinhua/ Getty Images, p. 45 (Chandrawati).